THE LITTLE BOOK OF

50 COCKTAIL RECIPES
FOR YOU TO MAKE AT HOME

© Mark Shorter

Contents

Contents

Equipment Needed

Mixing vessel

Cocktail shaker

Long spoon

Measurer

Tongs

Hawthorn strainer

Sugar syrup

Sugar syrups are used in quite a few of the cocktails, to make it just dissolve 300g caster sugar in 150ml water over a low heat. Leave to cool and bottle for future use. Store in the fridge.

Contents By Main Spirit

Sugar syrup

Sugar syrups are used in quite a few of the cocktails, to make it just dissolve 300g caster sugar in 150ml water over a low heat. Leave to cool and bottle for future use. Store in the fridge.

ESPRESSO MARTINI

10ml Sugar syrup
100ml vodka
50ml freshly brewed espresso coffee
50ml coffee liqueur
3 coffee beans (optional)

Origin

London
England

Method

First put a martini glass in the fridge to chill. Pour 1 tbsp of the sugar syrup into a cocktail shaker along with a handful of ice, the vodka, espresso and coffee liqueur. Shake until the cocktail shaker feels cold. Strain into the glass.

Garnish with the coffee beans.

Amaretto Sour[2]

**200ml amaretto
3-4 lemons, juiced (120ml)
1 egg white
small jar or can of cherries in syrup**

Method

Origin
Oregon
America

Put the amaretto, lemon juice, egg white and 4 teaspoons of the cherry syrup into a blender (without ice). Whizz up the mixture a few times at a high speed until it is pale and starting to increase in volume, Add a few handfuls of ice and pulse twice more to chill the mixture. Alternatively, stir in the ice until the outside of the jug feels cold, then pour into your glass

Garnish with a cocktail cherry.

LBV Portini

**100ml LBV (Late Bottled Vintage) Port
25ml Gin
25ml Campari**

Origin
Portugal

Method

Stir all the ingredients together in an ice filled glass.

Garish with a twist of orange peel.

Porn Star Martini

50ml vodka
50ml passion fruit puree
25ml passoa
1 tsp vanilla syrup (extract)
1 tsp lime juice
1 tsp sugar syrup
25ml prosecco or champagne

Origin

London
England

Method

Add the vodka, pasion fruit puree, passoa, lime juice and vanilla syrup to a cocktail shaker. Add a handful of ice and shake vigorously for about 20 seconds or until foamy. Strain into a martini glass, top up with prosecco or champagne.

Garnish with half a passion fruit.

Margarita

50ml tequila
25ml lime juice
20ml triple sec
salt
2 lime wedges

Method

Origin
Puebla
Mexico

Add a few teaspoons of salt into saucer. Rub one wedge of lime along the rim of a glass and then dip it into the salt so that the rim is covered. Fill a cocktail shaker with ice, add the tequila, lime juice and triple sec. Shake until the outside of the shaker feels cold.
Strain the mix into your prepared glass over fresh ice.

Garnish with a wedge or slice of lime.

Bellini

50ml peach purée
125ml prosecco

<u>**Origin**</u>
Venice
Italy

<u>**Method**</u>

Pour the peach purée
into a long stemmed
glass containing the
prosecco.

Garnish with a peach
slice.

Gin Basil Smash

**10 to 12 fresh basil leaves + extra for garnish
60ml London Dry gin
25ml freshly squeezed lemon juice
15ml sugar syrup**

Method

Origin
Hamberg
Germany

Muddle the basil leaves with the lemon juice in a shaker until the lemon juice turns a vivid green. Add the rest of the ingredients and some ice to the shaker and shake vigorously. Double strain the ingredients into an ice-filled glass.

Garnish with a basil leaf.

End Of The Rainbow

25ml Grenadine
100ml Pineapple Juice
50ml Coconut Rum
12.5ml Blue Curacao
25ml Ice cold water

Origin

No reference
Lots of variations

Method

Pour the grenadine into the bottom of a hurricane glass, then fill the glass with ice, combine the coconut rum and pineapple juice in a separate glass and then carefully pour over the ice, finally combine the Curacao and ice cold water together and gently pour on top of your drink.

Garnish with a cocktail cherry and a slice of orange.

French Martini

40ml vodka
20ml Chambord liqueur
60ml pressed pineapple juice
pineapple wedge, to serve

Origin
New York
America

Method

Shake the vodka, Chambord and pineapple juice with ice vigorously in a cocktail shaker until the juice froths up a small amount, then strain into your glass.

Garnish with the pineapple wedge if desired.

Kamikaze

30ml Vodka
30ml Triple sec
15ml lime juice

Origin
Tokyo
Japan

Method

Shake all the ingredients together with ice in a cocktail shaker until chilled, then strain into a martini glass.

Garnish with a twist of lime.

Manhattan

75ml bourbon
15ml sweet vermouth
15ml extra dry vermouth
2 dashes of Angostura bitters
5ml cherry brandy

Origin
Manhattan
America

Method

Pour all of the ingredients into a mixing glass, add a few ice cubes and stir. When mixed to the desired strength has been achieved, strain into a martini glass.

Garnish with a couple of maraschino cherries or a twist of orange zest.

Negroni

25ml gin
25ml sweet vermouth
25ml Campari

Origin

Milan
Italy

Method

Pour the gin, vermouth and Campari into a mixing glass with ice. Stir well until chilled.

Strain into a tumbler and add a few large ice cubes.

Garnish with an orange slice.

Paloma

**50ml tequila blanco
10ml agave syrup
10ml lime juice
60ml pink grapefruit juice
soda water**

Method

Origin
Tequila
Mexico

Add a few teaspoons of salt into saucer. Dip the rim of the glass in some water and then dip it into the salt so that the rim is covered. Fill a cocktail shaker with ice, then add all the ingredients except the soda water. Shake until chilled, then strain into a highball glass. Add a few fresh ice cubes and top with soda water to serve.

Garnish with the slice of grapefruit.

Aperol Spritz

Origin
Padua
Italy

Method

Add plenty of ice to a
glass and add the
Aperol, then add the
prosecco and top up
with soda, if you like.

Garnish with a slice of
orange.

Corpse Reviver

25ml dry gin
25ml Cointreau
25ml Lillet blanc
25ml lemon juice
2.5ml sugar syrup
2 dashes Absynth

Origin

London
England

Method

Shake all the ingredients together with ice in a cocktail shaker until chilled, then strain into a martini glass.

Garnish with a twist of lemon.

Sangria

25ml Spanish brandy
90ml Red wine
15ml Curaçao
10ml sugar syrup
10ml lemon juice
1tsp cinnamon
25ml soda water

Origin
Spain

Method

Mix all the ingredients except for the soda water in a balloon glass with ice, then top up with the soda water.

Garnish with strawberries, mint leaves and slices of orange and lemon.

Mai Tai

25ml golden rum
1 tbsp orange curacao
2 tsp orgeat syrup
25ml lime juice
2 tsp sugar syrup
25ml dark rum

Method

Pour all the ingredients except the dark rum into a cocktail shaker with a handful of ice cubes. Shake until the outside of the shaker is very cold.

Origin
California
America

Fill a glass with crushed ice and strain the cocktail over it. Slowly pour the dark rum over the top so it sits on the surface.

Garnish with pineapple, lime and cocktail cherries if you desire.

Swedish Polar Bear

50ml vodka
25ml curacao
100-150ml sprite to taste

Origin
Sweden

Method

Mix the vodka and curacao in a tall glass filled with ice, then top up with the sprite.

Garnish with a slice of lemon or orange.

Naked and Famous

22.5ml Mezcal
22.5ml yellow Chartreuse
22.5ml Aperol
22.5ml fresh lime juice

Origin
New York
America

Method

Fill a cocktail shaker with ice cubes. Add all of the remaining ingredients and shake until chilled. Strain into a chilled cocktail glass.

Garnish with a wedge of lime.

White lady

50ml gin
25ml triple sec
25ml lemon juice serve
2 tsp sugar syrup
1/2 egg white (optional)

Origin

London
England

Method

Add all the ingredients to a cocktail shaker. Shake until the outside of the shaker is really cold, then strain the mixture. Remove the ice, return the drink to the shaker and shake again until the egg white is frothy, then pour into a cocktail glass.

Garnish with a twist of lemon zest.

Baby Guinness

60 ml coffee liqueur chilled
30 ml Irish Cream liqueur chilled

Method

Origin
America

Fill a shot glass 2/3 full with coffee liquer.

Pour the Irish cream over the back of a spoon. It will layer on top of the coffee liqueur and form the head which makes it look like a mini Guinness.

Picante De La Casa

Red Jalapeno chilli (deseeded and chopped)
Coriander / Cilantro
60ml Patrón tequila
20ml Agave syrup
30ml lime juice

Origin
Hollywood
America

Method

Muddle the chilli and coriander/cilantro in a cocktail shaker, add ice and pour in the other ingredients, shake until chilled and then strain into a chilled tumbler glass.

Garnish with the head of the chilli.

Old Fashioned

2 tsp sugar syrup
1-2 dashes Angostura bitters
60ml Scotch whisky or bourbon
soda water (optional)

Origin
Louisville
America

Method

Mix the sugar syrup and
bitters in a tumbler glass.
Fill the glass with ice and
stir in the whisky.
Add a splash of soda
water if you like a mixer.

Garnish with a slice of
orange and a cherry.

Dry Martini

**2-3 green olives , pitted, plus
12.5ml of the brine
75ml London dry gin
12.5ml dry vermouth**

Origin
New York
America

Method

Put a martini glass in the fridge to chill. Thread olives onto a cocktail stick and set aside. Fill a mixing glass with ice, then pour in the gin, vermouth and olive brine. Stir until chilled. Taste to make sure you're happy with the dilution.
Strain the mix into the chilled glass.

Garnish with the olive skewers.

Cantaritos

60ml Patrón tequila
45ml orange juice
22.5ml pink grapefruit juice
15ml lime juice
50ml pink grapefruit soda
pinch of salt

Origin
Jalisco
Mexico

Method

Pour all the ingredients into a glass filled with ice and stir.

Garnish with a slice of lemon or orange.

Bramble

50ml gin
25ml lemon juice
3/4 tbsp sugar syrup
3/4 tbsp blackberry liqueur
crushed ice

Origin
London
England

Method

Shake the gin, lemon juice and sugar syrup in a cocktail shaker with a handful of ice cubes until chilled, strain into a tumbler full of crushed ice. Drizzle the blackberry liqueur over the top so it 'bleeds' into the drink.

Garnish with a lemon slice and blackberries if you have them.

Screaming Orgasm

15ml Vodka
15ml Amaretto
15ml Irish Cream
15ml Coffee Liqueur
45ml Milk

Origin
Paris
France

Method

Shake all the ingredients together in a cocktail shaker with a handful of ice until chilled. Strain over crushed ice into a cocktail glass.

Garnish with whipped cream and a cherry.

Bloody Mary

50ml vodka
250ml tomato juice
1/2 tbsp lemon juice
few shakes Worcestershire sauce
few shakes Tabasco sauce
pinch celery salt
pinch black pepper

Origin
Paris
France

Method

Add all the ingredients
to a mixing glass/jug
filled with ice, then
strain into a tall glass
filled with ice.

Garnish with a celery
stick and a wedge of
lemon or lime.

Vieux Carré

25ml rye whisky
25ml cognac
25ml sweet vermouth
1 tsp Benedictine
2 dashes Peychaud's Bitters
2 dashes Angostura bitters

<u>Origin</u>
New Orleans
America

<u>Method</u>

Stir all the ingredients together in a mixing glass with ice, then strain into a tumbler glass filled with ice.

Garnish with a twist of lemon.

Mojito

60ml white rum
15ml freshly squeezed lime juice
12.5ml sugar syrup to taste
small handful mint leaves
soda water or lemonade depending on
sweetness preference

Method

Origin
Havana
Cuba

Muddle the lime juice, sugar syrup and mint leaves in a small jug until the mint is crushed. Pour into a tall glass with a few lime cut into wedges and add a handful of crushed ice. Pour over the rum, stirring with a long spoon. Top up with soda water.

Garnish with mint and a slice of lime.

Piña colada

120ml pineapple juice
60ml white rum
60ml coconut cream

Origin
San Juan
Puerto Rico

Method

Pulse all the
ingredients with a
handful of ice in a
blender until
smooth. Pour into a
tall glass.

Garnish with a
wedge of pineapple
if desired.

The Last Word

30ml Dry gin
20ml Green Chartreuse
20ml Maraschino Liqueur
20ml lime juice

Origin
Detroit
America

Method

Shake all the ingredients together in a cocktail shaker with ice, shake until chilled and then strain into a cocktail glass.

Garnish with a twist of ice.

Zombie

25ml dark rum
25ml white rum
50ml lime juice
150ml pineapple juice
1 tsp grenadine

Origin

Hollywood
America

Method

Pour the rums and fruit juices into a cocktail shaker filled with ice and shake hard until chilled. Strain the mixture into a tall glass filled with ice, then slowly pour in the grenadine to colour the drink.

Garnish the drink with mint sprigs.

Long Island Ice Tea

12.5ml vanilla vodka
12.5ml London dry gin
12.5ml reposado tequila
12.5ml rum
12.5ml triple sec
12.5 - 25ml fresh lime juice
125ml cola
1/2 a lime, cut into wedges

Origin
New York
America

Method

Pour all the spirits into a mixing glass, add the lime juice to taste. Half fill the glass with ice, then stir until chilled. Add the cola then stir to combine.
Fill a tall glass with more ice cubes and pour in the iced tea.

Garnish with a slice of lime.

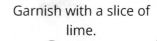

Whisky Sour

50ml bourbon
35ml lemon juice
12.5ml sugar syrup
2 dashes Angostura bitters
1/2 fresh egg white
50p size lemon zest

Method

Origin

Wisconsin
America

Shake all of the ingredients with ice in a cocktail shaker, strain into an ice-filled tumbler glass. Squeeze the lemon zest over the drink so the scented oils spray across the surface. Discard the zest.

Garnish with a slice of lemon and a cherry if desired.

Daquiri

50ml white rum
25ml lime juice
10ml sugar syrup

Origin

Santiago
Cuba

Method

Shake all the
ingredients in a
cocktail shaker with ice
and strain into a
cocktail glass.

Garnish with a wedge
of lime.

Slow Comfortable Screw Against The Wall

15 ml Galliano
15 ml Sloe gin liqueur
15 ml Southern comfort
45 ml Vodka
90 ml Orange juice

Origin
Variation of the
Screwdriver cocktail
America

Method

Mix the vodka, Southern comfort and orange juice in a mixing glass with ice, strain into a tall glass filled with ice, pour over the sloe gin so it bleeds through and top off with the Galliano.

Garnish with a slice of orange.

Gin Sour

60ml Dry gin
30ml Lemon juice
15ml Sugar syrup
15ml egg white
3 drops Angostura bitters

Origin
Toronto
Canada

Method

Add the gin, lemon juice, sugar syrup and egg white into a cocktail shaker with ice until chilled.Strain into a tumbler glass filled with fresh ice.

Garnish with a lemon twist and decorate the frothy top with 3 drops of Angostura bitters.

Americano

30ml Campari
30ml sweet red vermouth
soda water

Origin
Milan
Italy

Method

Pour all the ingredients into a tall glass full of ice and give it a gentle little stir to combine all the ingredients.

Garnish with an orange slice or two if using.

Hand Grenade

25ml Vodka
25ml White Rum
25ml Dry gin
37.5ml Melon Liqueur
25ml Rectified alcohol
Sugar Syrup
Pineapple Juice

Origin
New Orleans
America

Method

Pour all the
ingredients into a
cocktail shaker with
ice until chilled,
strain into a tall
glass filled with
crushed ice.

Fluffy Duck

30ml Triple Sec
30ml Orange Juice
45ml Advocaat
45ml Dry Gin
Soda Water

Origin
Unknown

Method

Add all the ingredients, except the soda water, to a cocktail shaker with ice and shake until chilled, strain into an ice-filled tall glass and top up with the soda water.

Garnish with an orange slice.

Tequila Sunrise

2 tsp grenadine
50ml tequila
1 tbsp triple sec
1 large orange, or 2 small ones, juiced
1/2 lime, juiced

Origin

California
America

Method

Pour the grenadine into the base of a tall glass and set aside. Fill a cocktail shaker with ice and add the rest of the ingredients, shake until cold. Add a few ice cubes to your glass and carefully strain the cocktail into it, try not to disturb the grenadine layer too much.

Garnish with a cherry or a cocktail umbrella.

Sex On The Beach

25ml vodka
12.5ml peach schnapps
25ml orange, juiced
25ml cranberry juice
25ml pineapple juice

Origin
Florida
America

Method

Pour the peach schnapps, orange juice and pineapple juice into a shaker with ice and shake until chilled. strain into an ice filled tall glass, then shake the vodka and the cranberry juice together and strain them over the top.

Garnish with a slice of orange.

STRAWBERRY DAQUIRI

250g strawberries, hulled
100g ice
50ml rum
juice 1/4 lime
1 tbsp sugar syrup, optional

Method

Blend the strawberries
and push the puree
through a sieve to
remove some
of the seeds.
Add the puree back to
the blender with all the
other ingredients, blend
and then pour into a
martini glass.

Serve with a fresh
strawberry and a sprig of
mint.

Moscow Mule

50ml vodka
100ml ginger beer
15ml lime juice
10ml sugar syrup

Origin
New York
America

Method

Pour the vodka, lime juice and sugar syrup into a tall glass filled with ice, pour over the ginger beer and stir.

Garnish with a a few wedges of lime.

Singapore Sling

50ml dry gin
12.5ml cherry brandy
12.5ml Benedictine
few drops Angostura bitters
50ml pineapple juice
15ml lime juice

Origin

Singapore

Method

Shake all the ingredients together with ice in a cocktail shaker until chilled, then pour into a tall ice filled glass.

Garnish with a wedge of pineapple and a cherry.

Gin Fizz

50ml gin
25ml lemon juice
2 tsp sugar syrup
soda water

Origin

New Orleans
America

Method

Pour the gin, lemon juice and sugar syrup into a cocktail shaker filled with ice. Shake well until very chilled, then strain into a tall glass filled with ice and top up with soda water.

Garnish with a lemon slice and mint.

Cosmopolitan

45ml lemon vodka
15ml triple sec
30ml cranberry juice
10ml lime juice

Origin
Minneapolis
America

Method

Shake all the
ingredients together
with ice in a cocktail
shaker until chilled,
then strain into a
martini glass.

Garnish with a twist
of lemon.

White Russian

60ml Vodka
30ml coffee liqueur
30ml cream

Origin
California
America

Method

Stir the vodka and coffee liqueur together in an ice filled glass, then carefully pour (float) the cream over the top.

Fruit Tingle

45ml Vodka
30ml Blue Curaçao
15ml crème de framboise
120-150ml lemonade

Origin
Australia

Method

Stir all the ingredients together in a tall cocktail glass filled with ice.

Garnish with a wedge of pineapple and a cherry.

YOUR OWN CREATIONS

Use the following pages to add your own cocktail recipes

THE LITTLE BOOK OF

Cocktails

© Mark Shorter

Printed in Great Britain
by Amazon